BEZALEEL

THE MAKING OF A SERVANT OF THE LORD

"Bezaleel made all that the LORD commanded Moses."
Exodus 38:22

ISBN: 979-8-9917801-6-2

Dr. Tom Sexton

Table Of Contents

Bezaleel

———— A Gift from God to Moses ————

The LORD said to Moses, "I have called by name Bezaleel...And I have filled him with the spirit of God, in wisdom, and in understanding, and in knowledge, and in all manner of workmanship... in the hearts of all that are wise hearted I have put wisdom, that they may make all that I have commanded thee...

And Bezaleel...made all that the LORD commanded Moses."

Exodus 31:1-6, 38:22

Bezaleel was a man God had readied for the next chapter in His plan for the ages. When it was time to build the Tabernacle, Bezaleel was ready. All God needed was for Moses to give his life to do His will.

God's will has not changed. He "is not willing that any should perish." He wants "all men to be saved, and to come unto the knowledge of the truth." II Peter 3:9; I Timothy 2:4. The Lord Jesus said, "The harvest truly is plenteous, but the labourers are few;" Matthew 9:37; and that we should pray for laborers.

★★★★★

What God did for Moses, in preparing Bezaleel, He is doing today. This book has been written to help awaken an army of men like Bezaleel.

Please read the thrilling story of Bezaleel.

Exodus 31-38

★ ★ ★ ★ ★

Life In Egypt

The life of Bezaleel the son of Uri, the son of Hur, of the tribe of Judah began in Egypt when he was born a slave. We know very little about the daily lives of the children of Israel except what God said to Moses at the burning bush meeting.

The Bible says, "And the angel of the LORD appeared unto him (Moses) in a flame of fire out of the midst of a bush: and he looked, and, behold, the bush burned with fire, and the bush was not consumed. And Moses said, I will now turn aside, and see this great sight, why the bush is not burnt.

And...God called unto him out of the midst of the bush, and said, Moses...*I am* the God of thy father, the God of Abraham, the God of Isaac, and the God of Jacob...And the LORD said, I have surely seen the affliction of my people which *are* in Egypt, and have heard their cry by reason of their taskmasters; for...the cry of the children of Israel is come unto me: and I have also seen the oppression wherewith the Egyptians oppress them.

Come now therefore...that thou mayest bring forth my people the children of Israel out of Egypt." Exodus 3:2-10.

★ ★ ★ ★ ★

We know the Egyptians were hard taskmasters. Life for Bezaleel was not easy.

Bezaleel like other young men, born slaves in Egypt, would have been holding onto the promises from God, given and repeated to him by his father and all the fathers before him, which God made to Abraham.

God said to Abraham, "And I will make of thee a great nation, and I will bless thee, and make thy name great; and thou shalt be a blessing: And I will bless them that bless thee, and curse him that curseth thee: and in thee shall all families of the earth be blessed." Genisis 12:2-3.

Bezaleel would have believed, like other young men of his day believed, that one day God would set them free. Meanwhile, he was under the Egyptian taskmasters. We know that Bezaleel was a very gifted young man.

God put in him "wisdom...understanding... knowledge, and...all manner of workmanship, To devise cunning works, to work in gold, and in silver, and in brass, and in cutting of stones, to set *them*, and in carving of timber, to work in all manner of workmanship." Exodus 31:3-5.

In other words, God had used these Egyptian master craftsmen, who were skilled in their craft, to teach and train Bezaleel. When Bezaleel left Egypt, he had in him a gift that Moses would need to do what God had given him to do.

★ ★ ★ ★ ★

The Bible says, "And Bezaleel the son of Uri, the son of Hur, of the tribe of Judah, made all that the LORD commanded Moses." Exodus 38:22.

Bezaleel's life in Egypt was not an easy life, but when he left Egypt what was in his heart made him a treasure for the ages.

What Bezaleel did with his life was priceless. We can only imagine the joy and sense of achievement Bezaleel and all who had a part in building the Tabernacle in the wilderness felt when it was completed, and the fire and presence of God filled the Temple.

Bezaleel's life in Egypt teaches us some powerful truths about how God works in our lives when we cannot understand why things seem so wrong.

Nothing touches our life without God knowing it.

God said to Moses, "I have surely seen the affliction of my people which *are* in Egypt and have heard their cry by reason of their taskmasters; for...the cry of the children of Israel is come unto me:" God knows what is going on in our life.

What touches our life comes through a loving Father's hand.

Jesus said, "I give unto them eternal life; and they shall never perish, neither shall any *man* pluck them out of my hand. My Father, which gave *them* me, is greater than all; and no *man* is able to pluck *them* out of my Father's hand." John 10:28-29.

★ ★ ★ ★ ★

We are kept by the power of God, and nothing touches our lives that does not come through a loving Father's hand.

What God allows, to touch our life, has the power to make us better.

The Bible says, "And we know that all things work together for good to them that love God, to them who are the called according to *his* purpose." Romans 8:28.

It sometimes takes a while to see and understand why things happen the way they do. But remember God says, "My thoughts *are* not your thoughts, neither *are* your ways my ways, saith the LORD. For *as* the heavens are higher than the earth, so are my ways higher than your ways, and my thoughts than your thoughts." Isaiah 55:8-9.

If we do not get bitter the Lord can use what we learn.

The Bible says, "In every thing give thanks: for this is the will of God in Christ Jesus concerning you." I Thessalonians 5:18.

It is easier to wait until life is lived and then look back to be thankful. However, the Bible says **"in"** everything give thanks not "after" everything is over.

Bezaleel must have been a joyful person, otherwise the master craftsmen of Egypt would not have invested their lives in him.

God Gives Bezaleel To Moses

"And the LORD spake unto Moses, saying, See, I have called by name Bezaleel the son of Uri, the son of Hur, of the tribe of Judah...and I, behold, I have given with him Aholiab, the son of Ahisamach, of the tribe of Dan: and in the hearts of all that are wise hearted I have put wisdom, that they may make all that I have commanded thee." Exodus 31:1-2,6.

Bezaleel was a gift from the Lord, given to Moses, who God said, will "make all that I have commanded thee." Exodus 31:6. In other words, Bezaleel had learned from the master builders in Egypt all that would be needed to help Moses do God's will on earth.

When we pray to God, "Thy will be done on earth as it is in Heaven," do we understand how the Lord has given men and women, who He has prepared, the skill set, and resources needed to help us carry out God's will on earth? Maybe that is one of the reasons much of what God wants done on earth is unfinished.

We need men like Bezaleel to help us carry out what the Lord has commissioned us to do.

Bezaleel's true gift was his ability to fashion beautiful works of gold and silver, that he had learned, while he was a slave in Egypt.

★ ★ ★ ★ ★   7

He would have been one of the men, the builders in Egypt, would have wished to stay in Egypt.

He was what we call a prodigy. Think about how God put in him all he would need to help Moses do what God wanted done in this world. He was a treasure yet to be discovered by God's people.

The Bible mentions approximately 3,237 different people. Some of the men and women who are mentioned did something amazing with their life, and some are only just mentioned. Bezaleel is one whose life was amazing. Bezaleel was one in a million and was a treasure that the nation of Israel would soon discover.

Studying the people that the LORD used to accomplish His plan and purpose, down through the ages, is one of my favorite methods of Bible study. The men and women of like passion who had a heart for God and His work, left behind a message for all to follow.

Bezaleel was one of those amazing men. He was not a preacher or prophet; he was a craftsman. He was, what we call today, a layman. Without Bezaleel the work of the LORD would have been hindered, and Moses would not have accomplished all that he did for the LORD.

As we study this remarkable young man, we will discover what all laymen need to help God's man do what He has called them to do. May the LORD give us some men like Bezaleel, who will use what the LORD has put in them to advance the cause of Christ.

★ ★ ★ ★ ★

There are several questions we must ask if we want to learn about Bezaleel:

- **Who was he?**
  Bezaleel was born a slave in Egypt. He would have learned from the master craftsmen in Egypt how to be a craftsman.

- **When did he live?**
  Bezaleel lived when Egypt was at its zenith. He lived when God's people were in bondage. He lived when God sent Moses to Pharaoh. He would have witnessed first-hand the next great event in God's plan for His chosen people. He lived in a fearful time in Egyptian history.

- **Did he face any challenges or difficulties in life?**
  The Egyptian taskmasters were very cruel. His life would not have been a life of ease. He also witnessed the collapse of a world power, Egypt. Because of his exceptional gifts and abilities, he could have chosen to remain in Egypt and not leave in the Exodus.

- **Who influenced his life?**
  Bezaleel was influenced by the craftsmen in Egypt and then influenced by Moses. Without Moses, Bezaleel would have lived and died, and no one would have known his name. One of God's greatest leaders touched his life and gave him the opportunity to use his gift for God.

★★★★★

- **What impact did he make in life?**
Bezaleel built the Tabernacle in the wilderness.

He personally trained many men and women in the work of the LORD. The testimony to Bezaleel that God gives, says it all.

The Bible says, "And Bezaleel the son of Uri, the son of Hur, of the tribe of Judah, made all that the LORD commanded Moses." Exodus 38:22. He helped Moses do what God put in his heart to do. Is there a greater purpose in life than helping people do God's will with their lives? What will be our epitaph? The objects Bezaleel fashioned are priceless.

Studying the life of Bezaleel and understanding who he was, when he lived, what challenges he faced, who influenced his life, and what he accomplished with his life, helps us see a bigger picture on how God works in every generation; and of course, how God is working in our lives today.

Give your life to do God's will, and God will show you His will for your life.

★ ★ ★ ★ ★

Lessons From His Life in Egypt

God knows what is going on in our lives.

The LORD truly does know our heartaches. He sees and hears our sorrows. The Bible says, "And the LORD said, I have surely seen the affliction of my people which are in Egypt and have heard their cry by reason of their taskmasters; for I know their sorrows" Exodus 3:7.

The Lord knows our pain and sorrows. The Bible says, "Casting all your care upon him; for he careth for you." I Peter 5:7.

Dr. Charles Weigle, the great song writer, wrote his most famous song because of a broken heart. This beautiful song was born in a night he cast all his brokenness on Jesus.

★ ★ ★ ★ ★

No One Ever Cared For Me Like Jesus

By *Charles Weigle*

I would love to tell you what I think of Jesus,

Since I found in Him a friend so strong and true.

I would tell you how He changed my life
completely;

He did something that no other friend could do.

Chorus

No one ever cared for me like Jesus;

There's no other friend so kind as He.

*No one else could take the sin and darkness from
me;*

O how much He cared for me.

All my life was full of sin when Jesus found me;

All my heart was full of misery and woe,

Jesus placed His strong loving arms about me

And He led me in the way I ought to go.

Every day He comes to me with new assurance;

More and more I understand His words of love.

But I'll never know just why He came to save me,

Till someday I see His blessed face above.

★ ★ ★ ★ ★

There are always two kingdoms that want you.

The LORD wants to use us, and the devil wants to use us. Which kingdom will we build? The Lord said, "See, I have called by name Bezaleel the son of Uri, the son of Hur, of the tribe of Judah" Exodus 31:2.

Jesus told Peter, "...Satan hath desired to have you..." Luke 22:31. The more someone means to God and His plan for the ages the more intense the spiritual battle will be over who uses them, the kingdom of God or the kingdom of this world.

God's kingdom is eternal, but the kingdoms of this world will all pass away.

So, "Love not the world, neither the things *that are* in the world. If any man love the world, the love of the Father is not in him. For all that *is* in the world, the lust of the flesh, and the lust of the eyes, and the pride of life, is not of the Father, but is of the world.

And the world passeth away, and the lust thereof: but he that doeth the will of God abideth forever." I John 2:15-17.

It's a dangerous love affair to fall in love with this world. The Bible tells us that when this happens in a believer's life, "the love of the Father is not in him." In other words, we lose the joy of loving Jesus and His touch on our life. Remember, "all that *is* in the world...passeth away."

Every life influences others – for good or bad.

The Lord said to Moses, "And I, behold, I have given with him Aholiab, the son of Ahisamach, of the tribe of Dan: and in the hearts of all that are wise hearted I have put wisdom, that they may make all that I have commanded thee." Exodus 31:6.

These two men, Bezaleel and Aholiab, were going to teach others how to do God's will in building the Tabernacle. The Bible says, God put in their hearts what they needed to teach others and how to help Moses do what God had given him to do. (Exodus 35:34)

Whose life are we influencing to do God's will? Every life is influencing someone. "For none of us liveth to himself, and no man dieth to himself." Romans 14:7.

People have a brief period to live.

God says to Moses, "See, I have called by name Bezaleel..." Exodus 31:2a. Bezaleel comes and goes, and we never hear of him again. He lived a brief moment in human history. But, in his life he did something eternal. He gave his life to do God's will and built the Tabernacle.

Life is very brief. The Bible says, "Whereas ye know not what shall be on the morrow. For what is your life? It is even a vapour, that appeareth for a little time, and then vanisheth away." James 4:14.

One day our journey will come to an end. The Bible says our life "is...a vapour, that appeareth for a little time, and then vanisheth away." What we do for the LORD, we must do quickly.

Make sure that you know Christ as your personal Saviour. John the Apostle said, "These things have I written unto you that believe on the name of the Son of God; that ye may know that ye have eternal life, and that ye may believe on the name of the Son of God." I John 5:13.

(If you have doubts about your salvation, turn to the chapter, **God Loves You**, and nail down you Salvation today.)

Give your life to do His will and then find out what you are here on earth to do, and "be ye not unwise, but understanding what the will of the Lord is." Ephesians 5:17.

★ ★ ★ ★ ★

★ ★ ★ ★ ★

The Calling Of Bezaleel

The LORD said, "I have called by name Bezaleel..."
Exodus 31:2.

What does it mean to be called by God? It means God has chosen you for a mission in life. He has a purpose and plan for your life. Jesus said, "Ye have not chosen me, but I have chosen you, and ordained you, that ye should go and bring forth fruit, and that your fruit should remain: that whatsoever ye shall ask of the Father in my name, **he may give it you**." John 15:16.

Notice the last five words in this great verse. Jesus said, "He (God) may give it you." He did not say He would give it "TO" you. He said, "He may give it you." God is giving you to a work. There is no "to" in the verse. Why?

Because Jesus wants His followers to know that God has a plan and purpose for every life and He wants to give **you** to it. The Christian life is not just about all God gives to us, it is also about what God gives through us and what He gives us to do.

Bezaleel was a gift from God, fully prepared by God in the shadows of Egypt, for such a time as this moment in God's plan for the ages.

★ ★ ★ ★ ★

God will show all those who are surrendered to Him, His calling for their life. He will show you where you fit in His plan for the ages.

The Bible says, "For ye see your calling, brethren, how that not many wise men after the flesh, not many mighty, not many noble, *are called*: But God hath chosen the foolish things of the world to confound the wise; and God hath chosen the weak things of the world to confound the things which are mighty; And base things of the world, and things which are despised, hath God chosen, *yea*, and things which are not, to bring to nought things that are: That no flesh should glory in his presence." I Corinthians 1:26-29.

And when we see it (your calling), we will have more of an understanding about the journey that brought us to His will. When Bezaleel found out what God wanted Moses to build and that he was to help Moses do it, he knew what his life's great purpose was.

Most men spend their lives searching for the answer to these three questions.
- Who am I?
- Where did I come from?
- Why am I here?

The answer to these three questions gives meaning to life and will help us see that every life has a great purpose.

★ ★ ★ ★ ★

It has been said that when you are born, you cry and others rejoice; but if you have lived a life of purpose, when you die others cry and you rejoice.

Bezaleel's life made others rejoice. He could say, "I know who I am, and I know where I came from, and I know why I am here."

It has been said, "To know God's will is life's greatest knowledge, and to do God's will is life's greatest success."

Bezaleel did the will of God with his life, and studying his life helps us see how the LORD prepares His children for a life of purpose. This is the only Bezaleel in the Bible. His name means, "God is protection." Bezaleel was one of a kind. He was unique.

We are God's crown of creation.

The Bible says, "God created man in his own image, in the image of God created he him; male and female created he them." Genesis 1:27. God made us in His image. That means that we were made to live forever. We are eternal beings. We will spend eternity somewhere.

And may I add that Adam was created for a purpose. The Bible says, "And the LORD God took the man, and put him into the garden of Eden to dress it and to keep it." Genesis 2:15. God gave man the responsibility of caring for His creation. Adam was a caregiver. It is in our DNA to care for God's

★ ★ ★ ★ ★   19

creation. You can give a child a puppy or a plant and they will try to care for it. No other creation cares for God's creation but humans.

We are all one of a kind.

The psalmist said, "I will praise thee; for I am fearfully and wonderfully made: marvellous are thy works; and that my soul knoweth right well." Psalm 139:14.

There are no two people just alike. Identical twins are not even identical. No two snowflakes are the same.

A little boy told his mother what he had learned in Sunday School, about how God had made people. She said, "God does not make junk. Children, you are not junk or a weirdo, as some in the world might say. You are just peculiar."

Peter reminded the first century believers that they were "a peculiar people." He said, "But ye *are* a chosen generation, a royal priesthood, an holy nation, a peculiar people; that ye should shew forth the praises of him who hath called you out of darkness into his marvellous light:" I Peter 2:9.

Bezaleel came from a line of good men.

The Bible says he was "the son of Uri, the son of Hur, of the tribe of Judah." His father and grandfather were faithful men. None of us just showed up. We all got here through a family.

The Bible says, "The steps of a *good* man are ordered by the LORD: and he delighteth in his way." Psalms 37:23. Bezaleel was a good man. Bezaleel came from a family of faithful men. We all have the power to start a family of faithful men.

Are we willing to let the LORD give us to a work?

Are we willing to let the Lord spend our life for His purpose? Paul said, "And I will very gladly spend and be spent for you; though the more abundantly I love you, the less I be loved." II Corinthians 12:15.

Jesus said, "For whosoever will save his life shall lose it; but whosoever shall lose his life for my sake and the gospel's, the same shall save it." Mark 8:35.

The only way to find out our life's purpose is to surrender. Paul said, "I beseech you therefore, brethren, by the mercies of God, that ye present your bodies a living sacrifice, holy, acceptable unto God, which is your reasonable service. And be not conformed to this world: but be ye transformed by the renewing of your mind, that ye may prove what is that good, and acceptable, and perfect, will of God." Romans 12:1-2.

God's will is "good...acceptable...and perfect."

The level of our Christian service will be determined by the depth of our personal surrender. How far we go in God's plan for our life will be determined

★ ★ ★ ★ ★   21

by our willingness to walk in the light God gives us. "Thy word is a lamp unto my feet, and a light unto my path.... if we walk in the light, as he is in the light, we have fellowship one with another, and the blood of Jesus Christ his Son cleanseth us from all sin." Psalms 119:105; I John 1:7.

We are here to do His will. What would happen if we, who know Christ as our personal Saviour, gave our lives to do his will? The only way to find God's will and His calling for your life is to give your life for His will. The will of God for our life is to help everyone else do the will of God with their lives.

What is God's will for all? He is, "...not willing that any should perish, but that all should come to repentance." II Peter 3:9b. He wants all men to be saved.

★ ★ ★ ★ ★

It's Your Move

Draw nigh to God and God will draw nigh to you,

If you want to be closer to God, then this is what you <u>must</u> do.

The first step is where the flesh puts up its greatest fight,

But we cannot be closer to God if we're not willing to do right.

"There hath no temptation taken you

but such as is common to man,"

But God, who is faithful, has provided for us a plan.

He demonstrated His love on Calvary,

He has nothing left to prove,

If you truly want to be closer to God,

Then dear friend, "It's your move."

Lay aside the sin that has bound you

and keep walking in the light,

"Looking unto Jesus," to make sure you have clear sight.

Worldly pleasures and their companions,

You will have to forsake,

Keep your eyes on Jesus,

He will show <u>you</u> the path to take.

In His presence we win every victory,

Evil from Him will flee,

When we're close to God on this journey,

"the Truth," shall sets us free.

★ ★ ★ ★ ★

★ ★ ★ ★ ★

The Filling Of Bezaleel

"And the LORD spake unto Moses, saying, See, I have called by name Bezaleel the son of Uri, the son of Hur, of the tribe of Judah: And I have filled him with the spirit of God, in wisdom, and in understanding, and in knowledge, and in all manner of workmanship..." Exodus 31:1-4

God put in Bezaleel what he needed in order to help Moses accomplish the mission he was given and to build the Tabernacle. What God did for Moses, He is doing in our day, but we fail to see it.

Jesus said, "The harvest truly is plenteous, but the labourers *are* few; Pray ye therefore the Lord of the harvest, that he will send forth labourers into his harvest." Matthew 9:37-38.

What we fail to see is how the Lord is preparing people to help us do the will of God with our life and mission. The Lord told Paul, "For I am with thee, and...I have much people in this city." Acts 18:10.

In other words, God had people who would stand with Paul when he needed them. God always does His part in filling His children to carry on His plan

★ ★ ★ ★ ★

for the ages. We must be willing to do our part if we are to discover them.

Our part is to accept the responsibility of doing what God has put in our heart to do. Bezaleel was ready to join team Moses. Bezaleel and the children of God were waiting on Moses to say "Yes" to God.

There is a great army of believers waiting on us to say "Yes" to God and His plan for our life. Then we will see the next step and chapter God has for us. The life of Bezaleel shows us how God prepares people for His work.

Finding the people God has prepared to help us on our mission is the duty and responsibility of every leader. One of the great blessings and joy, in serving the Lord, is to be able to say to these God filled people "who knoweth whether thou art come to the kingdom for *such* a time as this?" Esther 4:14.

Bezaleel was ready to be used in the next chapter of God's plan for the ages. Little did he know that all he went through in Egypt, would be what Moses needed to carry-on God's plan for the next chapter in human history.

A study of the life and work of Bezaleel unlocks a measure of wisdom and understanding in how God builds His servants.

The tabernacle in the wilderness was built by laypeople, and Bezaleel was a layman. The tabernacle was the place where God came down and met with His people.

God said to Moses, "I have surely seen the affliction of my people which *are* in Egypt, and have heard their cry by reason of their taskmasters; for I know their sorrows; And **I am come down to deliver them** out of the hand of the Egyptians, and to bring them up out of that land unto a good land and a large, unto a land flowing with milk and honey; unto the place of the Canaanites, and the Hittites, and the Amorites, and the Perizzites, and the Hivites, and the Jebusites." Exodus 3:7-8. God came down. (John 1:1-14)

Today the church is a place where people come and meet with God. Jesus said He would build His church in Matthew 16:18. However, church ministries are built by laypeople.

Churches have ministries where laypeople can engage in the Lord's work. Jesus wants all His followers to have a part in the mission of taking the Gospel to the ends of the earth.

★ ★ ★ ★ ★

"Cause me to hear thy lovingkindness in the morning; for in thee do I trust:

Cause me to know the way wherein I should walk; for I lift up my soul unto thee.

Deliver me, O LORD, from mine enemies: I flee unto thee to hide me.

Teach me to do thy will; for thou art my God: thy spirit is good; lead me into the land of uprightness."

Psalm 143:8-10

★ ★ ★ ★ ★

FILLED WITH THE SPIRIT OF GOD

The LORD said, "And I have filled him with the spirit of God…" Exodus 31:3

Why being filled with the Spirit of God is first.

Being filled with the spirit of God is first, because only God sees our future and knows what we need within us to do His will. Bezaleel could not see his future, but he wanted to do something for God with his gifts and abilities. God knew Bezaleel would be the man to help Moses do what God wanted done on earth. God knows our future and will put in us what we need to live life more abundantly.

Jesus, in His model prayer, taught us to pray, "Thy will be done in earth, *as it is* in heaven." Matthew 6:10. What God has in His heart in Heaven, He wants done on earth. The Tabernacle was in the heart of God and He put in Bezaleel all he needed to accomplish it.

Christians are filled with the Spirit of God when they are saved. However, the filling of the Holy Spirit helps us get all we need to do God's will.

"Now we have received, not the spirit of the world, but the Spirit which is of God; that we might know the things that are freely given to us of God." I Corinthians 2:12. The question is, "What does it mean to be filled with the Holy Spirit?"

★ ★ ★ ★ ★   29

Finding the answer to this question requires a measure of understanding on our part.

To be filled with the Holy Spirit means having God put in us what we need to accomplish His will with our life. God will fill us with everything we need, to do what we are willing to accept, for what He wants done on this earth.

How much of God's plan for man are we willing to accept; and then give an account of what we have done, when we meet Him at the Judgement Seat of Christ?

The Bible says, "For we must all appear before the Judgment Seat of Christ; that every one may receive the things *done* in *his body*, according to that he hath done, whether it be good or bad." II Corinthians 5:10.

Would it surprise you to learn that how much of God's Spirit, power, and understanding He puts in us, is determined by <u>our</u> willingness to surrender to Him, and accept His will to be done on earth as it is in Heaven?

In other words, how much of what God has for you do you want? How much of God's will are you willing to do? Your answer will reveal what kind of Christian you become, and how much of God's power He gives you.

Have you ever heard, "Knowledge is power"? "Wisdom" and "Understanding" are also powerful. If God fills you with <u>Knowledge</u>, <u>Wisdom</u>, and

Understanding, He has filled you with the Spirit of God.

Many of us have been taught by a Christian who had knowledge, wisdom, and understanding. If you have, then you have met a Spirit-filled Christian.

Is there a difference in a man who is filled with the Spirit of God and a man who is not filled with the Spirit of God?

The Bible says, "And be not drunk with wine, wherein is excess; but be filled with the Spirit." Ephesians 5:18. Is there a difference in a man drunk with wine and a man not drunk with wine? The answer to both questions is, "Yes!"

There is a difference in a person filled or not filled with the Spirit of God. There is a noticeable difference.

I asked Dr. Roberson (my beloved pastor) how one could tell if a person was filled with the Spirit of God. His answer was heart searching. He said, "It is easier to tell when a man is not filled with the Holy Spirit; he is restless, discontent, and has a lack of spiritual fruit in his life."

Upon that answer, I had to find a place alone and ask God to fill me.

The subject of "Being Filled with the Holy Spirit" cannot be fully covered in one lesson or one thousand lessons. My purpose in this lesson is to show some simple truths that all laymen need. Remember, Bezaleel was not a preacher; he was a layman who did a powerful work for God.

The questions I would like you to consider in this lesson are:

- What is the filling of the Spirit?

- Why is it so important in the life of all believers?

- How can someone be filled with the Spirit of God?

What does it mean to be filled with the Spirit?

First, what is the filling of the Holy Spirit? The LORD said, "And I have filled him with the spirit of God..." God filled Bezaleel with the Spirit of God, and He commands His followers to be filled with the Holy Spirit. God says in His Word, "And be not drunk with wine, wherein is excess; but be filled with the Spirit." In other words, we should know what it means to be filled with the Spirit of God, because if we are not filled with God's Spirit we are not right with the Lord.

The answer to this question has been under discussion for hundreds of years. I have heard this subject discussed by "dry as a desert" Bible teachers and zealous new believers who could not quote two verses on the subject.

R. A. Torrey, in his book, "Why God Used D. L. Moody," said D. L. Moody tried to explain it to some pastors in his day. Moody explained how much they needed to be filled with the Spirit of God and was very saddened by their response.

Curtis Hutson, my dear friend who is with the Lord, tried to illustrate it by using his wife, Jerrie, as an example and nearly died prematurely.

He said, "Being filled with the Spirit is having more of God. For example, when I got married, I got all of Jerrie, my wife, but now I have more of her." Everyone but Jerrie laughed.

Dr. Roberson said, "It is what makes the difference in men. Men and women who are used of God are filled with the Holy Spirit, and people who are not mightily used of the Lord are not filled with the Spirit of God." God filled Bezaleel so He could use Him.

We are born into the family of God by the Spirit.

The Bible says we are born, "not of blood, nor of the will of the flesh, nor of the will of man, but of God." John 1:12-13. Again, we read, "And you hath he quickened, who were dead in trespasses and sins" Ephesians 2:1.

Jesus said, "Verily, verily, I say unto thee, Except a man be born of water and of the Spirit, he cannot enter into the kingdom of God. That which is born of the flesh is flesh; and that which is born of the Spirit is spirit." John 3:5-6.

We are sealed by the Spirit.

The Bible says, "And grieve not the Holy Spirit of God, whereby ye are sealed unto the day of redemption." Ephesians 4:30. Have you experienced that spiritual birth?

So, what does it mean to be filled with the Spirit? Let me say this for now. To be filled with the Spirit means to be emptied of self and filled with God. Every area of our life has changed.

Why is it so important to be filled with the Spirit?

This is where the LORD begins. He first fills Bezaleel with the Spirit then the rest follows. The Bible says, "Now we have received, not the spirit of the world, but the Spirit which is of God; that we might know the things that are freely given to us of God." I Corinthians 2:12. The Holy Spirit knows what we need in order for us to do what God has given us to do. You cannot have what is next if you do not get what is first.

What is next for you? Do you believe that the LORD knows what you need next? God knew what was next for Bezaleel. Before he could have what, he needed, he needed to be emptied of self and filled with the Spirit. No one gets what is next from God, in the Lord's work, before they are prepared for it.

The Christian life is a building process. We are to add to our faith (II Peter 1:5-9). We do not know what

★ ★ ★ ★ ★

lies ahead in our future, but the Lord knows. He will put in us all we need to succeed in His will and work. He wants all believers to finish right. He says, "Better *is* the end of a thing than the beginning thereof: *and* the patient in spirit *is* better than the proud in spirit." Ecclesiastes 7:8.

Be filled with the Spirit of God and He will put in you what you need to finish strong.

Jesus said, "But seek ye first the kingdom of God, and his righteousness; and all these things shall be added unto you." Matthew 6:33. No wonder God said first, "I have filled him with the spirit of God..."

How can we be "Filled With The Spirit"?

We must understand, God takes what you give Him, cleanses what He takes, fills what He has cleansed and uses what He has filled. The first step in being filled with the Spirit is to empty self. This is done by dying to self. Paul said, "I am crucified with Christ: nevertheless, I live; yet not I, but Christ liveth in me: and the life which I now live in the flesh I live by the faith of the Son of God, who loved me, and gave himself for me." Galatians 2:20.

Ask God to cleanse you. The Bible says, "If we confess our sins, he is faithful and just to forgive us our sins, and to cleanse us from all unrighteousness." I John 1:9. God will not fill a dirty vessel. People do not want water from a dirty cup.

★ ★ ★ ★ ★   35

Ask God to fill and use you. Jesus said, "If ye then, being evil, know how to give good gifts unto your children: how much more shall your heavenly Father give the Holy Spirit to them that ask him?" Luke 11:13.

The people who make a difference are those who are filled with the Spirit of God. People who are filled are in one accord. "And when they had prayed, the place was shaken where they were assembled together; and they were all filled with the Holy Ghost, and <u>they spake the word of God with boldness.</u>" Acts 4:31.

Being filled with the Spirit of God unites believers in heart, soul, mind, and strength.

Jesus said, "And thou shalt love the Lord thy God with all thy **heart**, and with all thy **soul**, and with all thy **mind**, and with all thy **strength**: this is the first commandment." Mark 12:30.

Every time we read of the first century believers being in one accord, we see the Lord did a powerful work through them. They boldly gave the Gospel and "GREAT" grace was upon them.

The Bible says, "And when they had prayed, the place was shaken where they were assembled; and they were all filled with the Holy Ghost, and they spake the word of God with boldness.

And the multitude of them that believed were of one heart and of one soul: neither said any of them that ought of the things which he possessed was his own; but they had all things common. And with great power gave the apostles witness of the resurrection of the Lord Jesus: and <u>great grace was upon them all</u>." Acts 4:31-33.

Bezaleel, and all those who God filled with His Spirit, were bold workers and were touched with greatness.

God takes what you give Him.

He cleanses what He takes.

He fills what He has cleansed.

He uses what He has filled.

★★★★★

BEZALEEL, FILLED WITH WISDOM

The Lord said, "...I have filled him with...wisdom... and in the hearts of all that are wise hearted I have put wisdom, that they may make all that I have commanded thee." Exodus 31:3,6.

The Lord gives us a list of all that He put in Bezaleel. At the top of the list is "the Spirit of God...." This is the starting place for all who desire to be used of God.

The next on the list is "...wisdom...." In this lesson we will ask the Lord to give us wisdom in order to understand how He builds men.

The Bible says, "The LORD...made known his ways unto Moses, his acts unto the children of Israel." Psalm 103:6-7. Moses needed wisdom to be able to work with people. People are complicated and do not always work together without problems.

Moses was to lead this group of people that the Word of God calls "a mixed multitude...with them..." Exodus 12:38. It takes wisdom not "people skills" to work with a mixed multitude of people.

Bezaleel was going to need everyone to be engaged, in building what God had given Moses to do, if he were to succeed. Only the Spirit of God knows how much wisdom we need to work with all believers.

That is why the Bible says, "If any of you lack wisdom, let him ask of God, that giveth to all *men* liberally, and upbraideth not; and it shall be given him." James 1:5.

Men may be able to teach us some people skills, but only God can give us the wisdom we need to work with all of His children.

What is wisdom? Where does wisdom come from? Do we need wisdom today?

I know of no subject that is more important, to the child of God, than this subject of wisdom.

Wisdom prepares us to meet God.

"The fear of the LORD is the beginning of wisdom..." Proverbs 9:10. To fear the Lord does not mean to walk around thinking that God is going to kill us or do some horrible thing to us. To fear the Lord means that we are sober to the fact that one day, we will give an account of our life to Him.

All believers will one day appear before the Judgment Seat of Christ. The Bible teaches us that, "we must all appear before the judgment seat of Christ; that everyone may receive the things done in his body, according to that he hath done, whether it be good or bad." II Corinthians 5:10

Understanding the seriousness of that day gives wisdom. I want to have a good day that day.

I wrote in my Bible, many years ago, this statement, "I am for anyone who wants to help me have a good day at the Judgment Seat of Christ." People who truly love you, and who want God's best for you, want you to have a good day when you see Jesus.

They want you to hear Him say to you, "Well done thou good and faithful servant."

Wisdom helps put the things of life in proper order.

The Bible says, "For wisdom is better than rubies; and all the things that may be desired are not to be compared to it." Proverbs 8:11.

Bezaleel would have the wealth that it would take to build the Tabernacle, given through his hands. Before Bezaleel was given the treasures from Egypt, he was given wisdom from God. A man, with the wisdom from God, will not be turned by the riches of this world.

It takes wisdom to avoid the things the Lord says we should not love. He says "Love not the world, neither the things *that are* in the world. If any man love the world, the love of the Father is not in him. For all that is in the world, the lust of the flesh, and the lust of the eyes, and the pride of life, is not of the Father, but is of the world.

And the world passeth away, and the lust thereof: but he that doeth the will of God abideth forever." I John 2:15-17.

It takes wisdom to avoid the forbidden loves of this world, which are, "the lust of the flesh, and the lust of the eyes, and the pride of life."

Think about all the gifted people we have known, and heard about, who discovered too late the danger of falling in love with the world and what it offers. It takes wisdom not to give your heart to the things that will all pass away one day.

No wonder the Lord tells us to, "Keep thy heart with all diligence; for out of it are the issues of life." Proverbs 4:23.

Wisdom makes it possible to work with people.

God said to Moses, "In the hearts of all that are wise hearted I have put wisdom, that they may make all that I have commanded thee" Exodus 31:6. In the Bible, "people skills" are called wisdom. We need wisdom to work with the many different people in our churches.

- Wisdom prepares us to meet God.

- Wisdom keeps us from being captured by riches.

- Wisdom makes it possible to work with people.

Do you have wisdom? Do you need more wisdom? The Bible says, "If any of you lack wisdom, let him ask of God, that giveth to all men liberally, and upbraideth not; and it shall be given him." James 1:5.

★ ★ ★ ★ ★

Wise men know Christ as their personal Saviour.

The Bible says, "But we preach Christ crucified, unto the Jews a stumbling block, and unto the Greeks foolishness; But unto them which are called, both Jews and Greeks, Christ the power of God, and the wisdom of God." I Corinthians 1:23-24. Do you know Christ as your personal Saviour?

Wise men make good leaders.

We are to find men with wisdom to put in leadership. The Bible says, "Wherefore, brethren, look ye out among you seven men of honest report, full of the Holy Ghost and wisdom, whom we may appoint over this business." Acts 6:3.

We read a testimony of these men who were leaders. The Bible says, "And they were not able to resist the wisdom and the spirit by which he spake." Acts 6:10.

Wisdom comes from the One who indwells you. "But the anointing which ye have received of him abideth in you, and ye need not that any man teach you: but as the same anointing teacheth you of all things, and is truth, and is no lie, and even as it hath taught you, ye shall abide in him." I John 2:27.

A wise man is one who knows the Scriptures.

Paul said of Timothy, "And that from a child thou hast known the holy scriptures, which are able to make thee wise unto salvation through faith which is in Christ Jesus." II Timothy 3:15. Knowing the Scriptures delivers us from destruction.

The Bible says, "He sent his word, and healed them, and delivered them from their destructions." Psalms 107:20.

God says, "My people are destroyed for lack of knowledge..." Hosea 4:6.

Wise men work at winning others to Christ.

We read, "The fruit of the righteous is a tree of life; and he that winneth souls is wise...And they that be wise shall shine as the brightness of the firmament; and they that turn many to righteousness as the stars for ever and ever." Proverbs 11:30; Daniel 12:3.

Let The Lord Have His Way
In Your Life Every day,
There's No Rest,
There's No Peace,
Till The Lord Has His Way,
Place Your Life In His Hand,
Rest Secure In His Plan,
Let The Lord,
Let The Lord Have His Way.

★ ★ ★ ★ ★

BEZALEEL, A MAN WITH UNDERSTANDING

"And I have filled him with the spirit of God, in wisdom, and **in understanding**, and in knowledge, and in all manner of workmanship" Exodus 31:3,31

Bezaleel is the first person, in the Bible, that God said had understanding. This does not mean he was the first person who had understanding; he is just the first person where we are told that he had understanding.

Understanding means seeing how everything fits together; to be able to see the big picture. People with understanding can see the finished product and know how to use different people to get there.

Understanding makes it possible to work together. The more a person understands, the more valuable they are. This is true in the world, and it is certainly true in the Lord's work. Every church and ministry needs men, with understanding, in order for people to work together and to be in a spirit of one accord.

Moses could not have accomplished all that he did in life without enlisting the help of all the people who came out of Egypt. He needed someone who could work with many different types of people, skills, and backgrounds.

Bezaleel was the man who put everyone to work. He found a job for all to do. The men and women who followed his leadership helped Moses to accomplish what God had put in his heart to do.

We need men with understanding. Understanding is seeing the big picture of what God is doing and seeing how it all works together with the resources available. Understanding also makes it possible to know <u>what</u> people can do in the Lord's work and how we all fit together as a team.

Only the Lord can open our minds of understanding.

We read about when the Lord Jesus opened the minds of the disciples, which were on the road to Emmaus, who were turning their back on God. The Bible says, "Then opened He (Jesus) their understanding, that they might understand the scriptures." Luke 24:45.

The road to Emmaus was the wrong direction; it was taking them away from the place God wanted them to be. The reason they were on this road is because they did not understand what the Lord was doing. Without understanding we will be on the wrong path.

The measure of our understanding reveals the measure of our spiritual maturity. Paul said, "When I was a child, I spake as a child, I understood as a child, I thought as a child: but when I became a man, I put away childish things." I Corinthians 13:11.

Children have a hard time understanding. They cannot see the big picture of life. They live in a small world with a small mind of understanding. The same can be said of a child of God who has not matured in the Lord and remains a "babe in Christ." The Lord said that He wanted to bless Israel, but did Israel understand? Moses said to the people of God, "...Consecrate yourselves today to the LORD, even every man upon his son, and upon his brother; that he may bestow upon you a blessing this day." Exodus 32:29.

Do we understand how much He wants to bless us? Pray for understanding that, "the eyes of your understanding being enlightened; that ye may know what is the hope of his calling, and what the riches of the glory of his inheritance in the saints" Ephesians 1:18. In Paul's prayer, for the people in the church at Ephesus, he asked the Lord to open their minds of understanding.

They had been given a great opportunity, and the door was open to them, but they had to see the big picture in order to see the door.

In our text, Moses has led the children of Israel out of Egypt, and now the next chapter in God's plan for the ages is about to unfold. Moses needed someone to help him who understood what God was doing. Bezaleel (a layman) was that man.

We, who know the LORD, understand that He has more to be accomplished on this earth. If this were not true, the Rapture would have taken place. It is the responsibility of all who lead to discover what God has in His heart to be done.

God will always give men like Bezaleel, to a leader who is given to doing the will of God with his life. Remember that God has promised to "supply all your need according to his riches in glory by Christ Jesus." Philippians 4:19. The greatest need in the Lord's work is laborers.

★★★★★

BEZALEEL, FILLED WITH KNOWLEDGE

"And Moses said unto the children of Israel, See, the LORD hath called by name Bezaleel the son of Uri, the son of Hur, of the tribe of Judah; And he hath filled him with the spirit of God, in wisdom, in understanding, and in knowledge, and in all manner of workmanship" Exodus 35:30-31.

As we continue our study in the life of Bezaleel, we see that he is filled "...in knowledge...." There are no shortcuts to getting knowledge. You must work at it.

Bezaleel is going to oversee the construction of the Tabernacle in the wilderness. He will be working with many different skilled men and women. He must know what they need to accomplish their part in God's plan.

He is filled with the Spirit of God. He has the wisdom to work with the different types of people and an understanding of how everything fits together, but he must have knowledge to know what everyone needs to do their part. The Lord knew what was ahead for Bezaleel. If Bezaleel were to succeed in life, he must be complete. He must have knowledge. How does someone get knowledge?

Find someone with knowledge.

The Bible says, "The lips of the wise disperse knowledge: but the heart of the foolish doeth not so." Proverbs 15:7. All who are wise have found someone with wisdom (knowledge) to teach them.

"Wise men lay-up knowledge..." (Proverbs 10:14) for the next generation. Bezaleel's life had crossed the path of those who had knowledge. You can learn from the world without loving the world. Remember the Lord is the source of all knowledge. The Bible says, "...The LORD is a God of knowledge, and by him actions are weighed." I Samuel 2:3.

Be the kind of person others want to teach.

"The simple inherit folly: but the prudent are crowned with knowledge." Proverbs 14:18. No one wants to teach a know-it-all. Be a reasonable man; use good judgment when working with others. Bezaleel would have been a pleasure to work with – a reasonable young man with personal discipline. People want to teach men with character.

Master the basics.

The Bible says, "For when for the time ye ought to be teachers, ye have need that one teach you again ..." Hebrews 5:12. You must have a good foundation in order to build a future. Men who do not master the basics do not become master builders. What are the basics of the Christian life? Work at becoming a Five Star Christian.

We need others to help complete the work God gives us.

★ ★ ★ ★ ★

"...The eye cannot say unto the hand, I have no need of thee: nor again the head to the feet, I have no need of you." I Corinthians 12:21.

There is no one that is good at everything. Know where people fit in God's work. Do not put a square person in a round hole or a round person in a square hole.

Accept people for where they are.

"Nay, much more those members of the body, which seem to be more feeble, are necessary" I Corinthians 12:22-25. People will do their best for those who see their worth. A person who gets the credit for the job must reflect honor to others. "Render therefore to all their dues: tribute to whom tribute is due; custom to whom custom; fear to whom fear; honour to whom honour." Romans 13:7.

Be a team player.

"For we are labourers together with God: ye are God's husbandry, ye are God's building." I Corinthians 3:9. You can be on the team and not be a team player. Some use others to make themselves look better, and some use their talent and gifts to make others better.

Remember it is a privilege to work with God's man.

"... They may make all that I have commanded thee" Exodus 31:6. When it is all said and done, only one person will give an account of the local church and all its ministries. "Obey them that have the rule over you, and submit yourselves: for they watch for your souls, as they that must give account, that they may do it with joy, and not with grief: for that is unprofitable for you." Hebrews 13:17.

It is the Lord's name that must be remembered. "That all the people of the earth may know that the LORD is God..." I Kings 8:60. Do we want all the people of the earth to know God, or to know us?

Do we have what it takes?

The Bible says, "Through wisdom is an house builded; and by understanding it is established: And by knowledge shall the chambers be filled with all precious and pleasant riches." Proverbs 24:3-4.

Three words in our text helps us to know what God is looking for in the people He uses to accomplish His work. He looks for people with knowledge, wisdom and understanding. Do we have what God is looking for? Do we have what it takes to continue the mission God has given us?

My beloved pastor, Dr. Lee Roberson, was one such man. He often said, "Everything rises and falls on leadership."

I learned from him that a leader is not someone who lords over people or controls their every move, but is someone who accepts responsibility for the mission God has given them. A leader is also someone who is willing to let other believers use their gifts and abilities to help them.

★ ★ ★ ★ ★

One of the great truths I learned from Dr. Roberson was to believe that every Christian we meet can have a part in what the Lord Jesus has given us to do. We must find a way for all of God's people to invest their lives in the Lord's work.

Not every church member is a "bullseye" Christian, but every child of God can, at some level, have a part in God's plan for the ages.

We need men and women with "knowledge."

First, they must know God. Paul said, "That I may know Him, and the power of His resurrection," Philippians 3:10. Do you know the Lord Jesus as your personal "Saviour?" This is where we all must begin.

Second, they must know God's Word. The Bible says, "My people are destroyed for lack of knowledge" Hosea 4:6. We need to have a firm grip on God's Word and God's Word needs to have a firm grip on us.

Third, they must know the challenges they are facing. The Bible says, "the children of Issachar, ...which were men that had understanding of the times, to know what Israel ought to do." I Chronicles 12:32.

God is looking for believers who know what is going on. He wants us to see the big picture.

We need men and women with "wisdom."

"Wisdom" is the ability to work with people who have "knowledge." I used to think that what believers needed were "people skills" to work with other people, but now I know that "people skills" is not Biblical. God's people need "wisdom."

One thing God tells us about Moses is, "Moses was learned in all the wisdom..." Acts 7:22.

In other words, he knew how to work with people, all people. The good news is, "If any of you lack wisdom, let him ask of God, that giveth to all men liberally," James 1:5.

We need men and women with "understanding."

"Understanding" is seeing the big picture of what God is doing and seeing how it all works together with the resources available. "Knowledge" is not enough. You must know Jesus and His Word. "Wisdom" is not enough. We must put "knowledge" to work.

Believers who have "understanding" of the times we live in, and "knowledge" of what needs done, will be given the "wisdom" to work with people.

Paul prayed for the believers in the church at Ephesus to receive, "knowledge, wisdom, and understanding." Ephesians 1:17-18.

★ ★ ★ ★ ★   53

"People must have some intrinsic worth, or God would not care so tenderly for them, they increase in value after they are saved."

★ ★ ★ ★ ★

BEZALEEL, FILLED WITH
ALL MANNER OF WORKMANSHIP

"And I have filled him with the spirit of God, in wisdom, and in understanding, and in knowledge, and in all manner of workmanship." Exodus 31:3.

There is no short cut in learning a skill or trade. Bezaleel would have learned from the master builders of Egypt, the skill set he needed to build the Tabernacle in the wilderness. Little did they know that one day this young man would be used to help one of the greatest leaders achieve success.

In the life of Bezaleel, we see a believer and his work. The word "work" is a four-letter word that most Christians do not like. When they hear the word, they have a negative reaction. We are saved by grace, but we are saved "unto good works..." Ephesians 2:10.

There is a job for every believer. There should be no unemployment in the Lord's work. Bezaleel had the responsibility of helping everyone find their place of service. He had to find where people fit in the building of the Tabernacle.

The goal of every leader, in the work of the Lord, is to help people find their place in the great work the Lord has given them. The golden rule in a church should be to accept people where they are, win them to Christ, and help them find something to do for our coming Saviour.

★ ★ ★ ★ ★   55

There is a work for all believers. The reason we say that is because the Bible says, "Every man's work shall be made manifest: for the day shall declare it, because it shall be revealed by fire; and the fire shall try every man's work of what sort it is." I Corinthians 3:13.

If every man's work is going to be tried, then it stands to reason that every man has a work. Serious minded believers live with "that day" in their hearts and minds. The day we meet the Lord Jesus and give an account of our life and work; is the most sobering thought a Christian can have.

I am for anyone who wants me to have a good day that day. We must "...believe..." that the Lord has something for us. The work of believers is to believe. The Lord Jesus was asked by the religious leaders, "What shall we do, that we might work the works of GOD?" He answered and said unto them, "This is the work of God, that ye believe on him whom he hath sent." John 6:28-29.

Jesus did all the work for our redemption, our work is to believe.

The church has been commissioned by God.

The Bible says, "Go ye therefore, and teach all nations, baptizing them in the name of the Father, and of the Son, and of the Holy Ghost: Teaching them to observe all things whatsoever I have commanded you: and, lo, I am with you alway, even unto the end of the world. Amen." Matthew 28:19-20.

The work of the Lord is to be carried out through the ministry of the local church. The church is on a mission from God.

Our mission is to preach the Gospel around the world.

Jesus said unto them, "Go ye into all the world, and preach the gospel to every creature." Mark 16:15. We are to make sure that every person hears the Gospel of Christ. We are not to leave one person out. We are to publish the Gospel in every nation. Jesus said, "And the gospel must first be published among all nations." Mark 13:10. We are on a mission from God to take the Gospel to all people.

Our mission is to go to four areas at the same time.

Jesus said to His followers, "But ye shall receive power, after that the Holy Ghost is come upon you: and ye shall be witnesses unto me both in Jerusalem, and in all Judaea, and in Samaria, and unto the uttermost part of the earth." Acts 1:8.

The little word "...both..." means "at the same time." The same people who are responsible for Jerusalem are responsible for the other areas. The church is to make sure that every area is covered. The Lord is looking for workers.

★ ★ ★ ★ ★

What does the Lord require of workers?

"What doth the LORD thy God require of thee, but to fear the LORD thy God, to walk in all his ways, and to love him, and to serve the LORD thy God with all thy heart and with all thy soul," Deuteronomy 10:12.

Live above reproach.

The Bible says, "Abstain from all appearance of evil." I Thessalonians 5:22.

Every worker should be a practicing, Christian. By that I mean that Christians should practice what they believe every day, not just on the Lord's Day.

Stay in one accord with other believers.

The Bible says, "And when the day of Pentecost was fully come, they were all with one accord in one place...And they, continuing daily with one accord in the temple, and breaking bread from house to house, did eat their meat with gladness and singleness of heart" Acts 2:1,46.

Staying in fellowship and one accord creates a powerful spirit in a church. This is the secret to having God's blessings. Every time we read "of one accord" in the Bible, there is a great moving of God in the church. Just one person can hurt the spirit of a church.

Stand with leadership.

Paul said in an hour when he was forsaken by others, "the LORD stood with me and strengthened me" II Timothy 4:17. People sometimes say, "I'm behind you, Preacher." I often remind them of what Jesus said to Peter, "...Get thee behind me, Satan...." I tell them, "Do not stand behind; stand beside me. If you stand beside me we will both get shot." Stand with leadership.

Keep the sunny side up.

"In every thing give thanks: for this is the will of God in Christ Jesus concerning you." I Thessalonians 5:18.

The little word "...in..." is the key to understanding this verse. We would change that word to "after." It is hard to give thanks while in trouble or heartache.

Anyone can look back and give thanks, but it takes a mature Christian to give thanks in problems and disappointments. Be a believer that lifts the spirits of others. Remember the joy of the Lord is still our strength (Nehemiah 8:10).

Be faithful.

The Bible says, "Moreover it is required in stewards, that a man be found faithful." I Corinthians 4:2. Determine to be faithful. You may not be the best singer or teacher or anything else, but you can always be faithful.

★ ★ ★ ★ ★

"Trained Workers Are A Ministry's

Greatest Asset."

★ ★ ★ ★ ★

Bezaleel And The Adversary
A Battle for Bezaleel

"And when the people saw that Moses delayed to come down out of the mount, the people gathered themselves together unto Aaron, and said unto him, Up, make us gods, which shall go before us; for as for this Moses, the man that brought us up out of the land of Egypt, we wot not what is become of him. And Aaron...made it a molten calf: and they said, These be thy gods, O Israel, which brought thee up out of the land of Egypt.

And when Aaron saw it, he built an altar before it; and Aaron made proclamation, and said, "Tomorrow is a feast to the LORD. And they rose up early on the morrow, and offered burnt offerings, and brought peace offerings; and the people sat down to eat and to drink, and rose up to play... and Moses saw that the people were naked." Exodus 32:1-8,25.

The Devil was behind this rebellion, and Aaron fell right into the trap. The Bible tells us to, "Be sober, be vigilant; because your adversary the devil, as a roaring lion, walketh about, seeking whom he may devour" I Peter 5:8.

On the eve of God doing something wonderful, in a believer's life, our adversary the Devil will do

★★★★★ 61

something to take our heart out of what God has planned for us to do.

In this three-part lesson we will see how the devil works to destroy the influence and character of God's people. And we will see how he discourages the hearts of leaders.

Bezaleel was a man who had been prepared by the LORD to help Moses accomplish the great work God had given him to do. Moses is excited to begin the next chapter God has for him. This rebellion is an attack on the next great chapter the Lord has for His people.

The two people who cannot get discouraged and sidetracked by this rebellion are Moses and Bezaleel. Moses has been through the fires to get to this place in his life, but Bezaleel must not get captured by this rebellion. The more someone means to God and His man, the more determined the evil one is to devour him.

If Moses was to build the Tabernacle in the wilderness, he needed Bezaleel.

God has Bezaleel ready, but Satan has a way to stop him. What the Devil used on Bezaleel is the same thing he uses on God's people today. How many times have we seen people, who were ready to take the next step with the LORD in His plan, fall prey to the adversary?

I have learned that we rarely see the big picture of Satan's plan to destroy the lives of God's gifted people; but here we know what the Devil's goal was in this rebellion. It is a threefold attack on believers. It is an attack on these who hold truth on the inward parts of their life.

This is a battle for Bezaleel. It is an attack on Moses and an attack on Bezaleel. Both Moses and Bezaleel have something God has put in their hearts to do for Him, and the devil tries to devour it.

- First, it is to get God's people to criticize their spiritual leadership. The people said, "as for this Moses." What contempt they had for Moses!

- Second, it is to get God's people to compromise their convictions. The Bible says, "the people were naked." They were acting like the Egyptians and the world.

- Third, it is to get God's people to cash in their God given gifts and abilities. "And Aaron... made...a molten calf." Aaron made it not Bezaleel, who could have made a real work of art.

Bezaleel must move past this trap before he will be able to do what God has called him to do. Bezaleel is a good man. The Devil wants good men to turn their backs on God. The Devil lays a trap for the good man.

"But know this, that if the goodman of the house had known in what watch the thief would come, he would have watched, and would not have suffered his house to be broken up." Matthew 24:43.

If you are a good man, then know "...Satan hath desired to have you..." Luke 22:31. The more we mean to God and His plan, the more intense the battle with evil will be in our life. Because of the seriousness of this lesson, I have divided it into three parts. How does Satan attack the child of God? In this case how did Satan attack Bezaleel?

WILL BEZALEEL BECOME CRITICAL OF MOSES?

"And when the people saw that Moses delayed to come down out of the mount, the people gathered themselves together unto Aaron, and said unto him, Up, make us gods, which shall go before us; for as for this Moses, the man that brought us up out of the land of Egypt, we wot not what is become of him." Exodus 32:1.

The first area that Bezaleel will be tested is in the area of criticism. Look how quickly the people became critical of Moses. "As for this Moses..." What a way to talk about God's man! You can feel the contempt in their voices.

Moses is receiving something from God for them, yet they are still critical of him. If Bezaleel joins in, then he is finished. They criticized Moses because they did not understand his relationship with God. Moses is God's man, and Satan is behind this criticism of him and his leadership.

The Bible says, "Who can stretch forth his hand against the LORD'S anointed, and be guiltless?" I Samuel 26:9. It is a very dangerous thing to touch God's man or His leadership with our tongue (I Timothy 5:19). Never give ear to criticism of leadership. Be careful about surrounding yourself with critical people.

★ ★ ★ ★ ★

"Let the words of my mouth, and the meditation of my heart, be acceptable in thy sight, O LORD, my strength, and my redeemer." Psalm 19:14

Criticism Always Weakens Leadership and The Ability To Help People In Their Time Of Need

The Bible says, "And Moses besought the LORD his God, and said, LORD, why doth thy wrath wax hot against thy people, which thou hast brought forth out of the land of Egypt with great power, and with a mighty hand?" Exodus 32:11.

Moses is the only one who can help them. They have destroyed his influence with their tongue. Often when young people are attacked by the evil one and his forces, the only people who could help them have been destroyed by criticism.

The LORD Does Not Use Critical People

The psalmist said, "Let the words of my mouth, and the meditation of my heart, be acceptable in thy sight, O LORD, my strength, and my redeemer." Psalm 19:14. Our words reflect our heart. If our heart is not right with God and others, our words will reveal it.

The Word of God teaches us that our tongue is the hardest member of our body to keep under control. The Bible says, "But the tongue can no man tame; it is an unruly evil, full of deadly poison." James 3:8.

Our tongue can start a fire that will burn up every good thing around us. You will not find in the Word of God, or in church history, God using anyone who became critical of leadership. If Bezaleel joins in the criticism of Moses, he is finished.

The Power Of Words

Here are four truths that all believers should know about their words.

Our Words Reflect Our Hearts

Jesus said, "A good man out of the good treasure of the heart bringeth forth good things: and an evil man out of the evil treasure bringeth forth evil things. But I say unto you, That every idle word that men shall speak, they shall give account thereof in the day of judgment." Matthew 12:35-36.

If we want to change our words, we must let the LORD change our heart. The Bible says, "Create in me a clean heart, O God; and renew a right spirit within me." Psalm 51:10.

Our Words Have Power

The Bible says, "Death and life are in the power of the tongue: and they that love it shall eat the fruit thereof." Proverbs 18:21. Our words have the power of death or life. The more influence someone has, the more powerful their words are.

People With Wisdom Are Careful With Their Words

The Bible says, "He that hath knowledge spareth his words: and a man of understanding is of an excellent spirit. Even a fool, when he holdeth his peace, is counted wise: and he that shutteth his lips is esteemed a man of understanding." Proverbs 17:27-28.

Our wisdom and maturity in the LORD is measured, in part, by our words.

Paul said, "When I was a child, I spake as a child, I understood as a child, I thought as a child: but when I became a man, I put away childish things." I Corinthians 13:11.

It Is The Duty Of All Believers To Encourage Someone Every Day

The Bible says, "But exhort one another daily, while it is called To day; lest any of you be hardened through the deceitfulness of sin." Hebrews 3:13. If our goal is to encourage someone every day, we will not be a discouraging person. Make this one of your "daily duties."

Taming The Tongue

"The tongue is a little member, and boasteth great things. Behold, how great a matter a little fire kindleth!

And the tongue is a fire, a world of iniquity: so is the tongue among our members, that it defileth the whole body, and setteth on fire the course of nature; and it is set on fire of hell.
For every kind of beasts, and of birds, and of serpents, and of things in the sea, is tamed,
and hath been tamed of mankind:

But the tongue can no man tame; it is an unruly evil, full of deadly poison."

James 3:4-8

★ ★ ★ ★ ★

WILL BEZALEEL COMPROMISE HIS CONVICTIONS?

"And they rose up early on the morrow, and offered burnt offerings, and brought peace offerings; and the people sat down to eat and to drink, and rose up to play… and Moses saw that the people were naked." Exodus 32:6,25.

The second area that Bezaleel will be tested is in his personal convictions. Will he join in and "eat, drink, and play naked?" Moses is out of sight, and many are joining in on this golden calf idol worship. The LORD told Moses that the people "…have corrupted themselves." Exodus 32:7. Has Bezaleel corrupted himself? No. He did not join in their rebellion. People who compromise their personal convictions lose the life they could have had.

It takes a while for people to develop their personal convictions. We live in a changing world, and many churches and Christians are changing with the world. We have many "Lot-minded believers" living in a "Gomorrah-minded world."

Our Personal Convictions Should Be Based on the Bible

The Bible says, "For ever, O LORD, Thy word is settled in heaven." Psalm 119:89. God's Word will not change. What the first-century believers believed should be the same things that we believe. We should earnestly commit to every generation,

"And the things that thou hast heard...the same commit to faithful men," II Timothy 2:2. If we change one thing, it is not the same. It has been said, "Things that are different are not the same.

Personal Convictions Help Us Stay Right And On Track

The Bible says, "For thou art my rock and my fortress; therefore, for thy name's sake lead me, and guide me...Thou shalt guide me with thy counsel, and afterward receive me to glory." Psalm 31:3; 73:24.

Two of the most difficult things to do in the Christian life are to stay right with God, and to stay on track with our life. Personal convictions based on God's Word helps us to accomplish these two things.

Developing Personal Convictions

Here are four truths that help us to know what is right and to stay on track.

Is It Pleasing To The LORD?

Jesus said, "And He that sent Me is with Me: the Father hath not left Me alone; for I do always those things that please Him." John 8:29. The highest goal of the Christian life is to please the LORD. The LORD Jesus said, "...I do always those things that please Him." If it does not please God, do not do it!

★ ★ ★ ★ ★

Will It Hinder My Walk And Witness For Christ?

The Bible says, "Wherefore seeing we also are compassed about with so great a cloud of witnesses, let us lay aside every weight, and the sin which doth so easily beset us, and let us run with patience the race that is set before us" Hebrews 12:1.

We do not want to pick up extra weight or sin. We are in a race. The LORD would never lead His children to pick up something that will hinder their race. We want to be a faithful witness. The LORD would not lead His children to pick up something that would limit our witness. If it will slow us down or limit our witness, say, "No!"

Can I Thank God For It And Put My Heart In It?

The Bible says, "And whatsoever ye do in word or deed, do all in the name of the Lord Jesus, giving thanks to God and the Father by him...And whatsoever ye do, do it heartily, as to the Lord, and not unto men." Colossians 3:17,23.

Enthusiasm and excitement are the spark in the work of the LORD. People will follow excited people. We will not have excitement or joy if we cannot thank God for it and put our whole heart into it. If you cannot thank God for it and put your heart into it, do not do it!

Is There Doubt Concerning It?

The Bible says, "And he that doubteth is damned if he eat, because he eateth not of faith: for whatsoever is not of faith is sin." Romans 14:23. There will always be that element of faith an unknowing, but doubt is a red light. Wait until the LORD gives you the green light. If your heart is right with God and you have strong doubt, wait! These four Bible truths will save you from a lot of heartache and disappointment.

★ ★ ★ ★ ★

WILL BEZALEEL USE HIS GIFT TO MAKE THE GOLDEN CALF?

The people said, "...Up, make us gods...And all the people brake off the golden earrings which were in their ears, and brought them unto Aaron. And he received them at their hand, and fashioned it with a graving tool, after he had made it a molten calf: and they said, These be thy gods, O Israel, which brought thee up out of the land of Egypt." Exodus 32:1-4.

The most gifted craftsmen in all of Israel is Bezaleel. He has been taught, by the masters in Egypt, how to fashion works of gold. He did not make this golden calf. The world wants what you have been given from God for their own lusts.

In the book of Daniel, we read that Nebuchadnezzar, who is a type of the Devil, wanted, "Children in whom was no blemish, but well favoured (this describes Christians) ... whom they might teach the learning and the tongue of the Chaldeans." Daniel 1:4.

The world wants the best and the best is God's people. The world wants you. They want your gifts and abilities to be spent on them. Sadly, we see and hear of those who grew up in church, singing in the choir or working in the ministry, cashing in for what the world will give them.

The world, and the lust thereof, will one day pass away (I John 2:15-17).

How can we help believers say "No" to all that the world offers them? How can we help them use their gifts and abilities for the LORD and His work?

Understand That Our Gifts And Abilities Are From God

The Bible says, "Every good gift and every perfect gift is from above, and cometh down from the Father of lights, with whom is no variableness, neither shadow of turning." James 1:17. We are not our own. There are no self-made men in the LORD's work. We are "...His workmanship, created in Christ Jesus unto good works..." Ephesians 2:10.

Believe That One Day We Will Give An Account Of Our Life To Him

The Bible says, "For we must all appear before the judgment seat of Christ; that every one may receive the things done in his body, according to that he hath done, whether it be good or bad." II Corinthians 5:10. Our work will one day be tried by fire to see of what sort it is.

The Bible says, "If any man's work abide which he hath built thereupon, he shall receive a reward." I Corinthians 3:14. Every man should find a place of service in his local church (Matthew 28:19-20).

★ ★ ★ ★ ★   75

Using Your Gifts For God

The Bible says, "Every good gift and every perfect gift is from above, and cometh down from the Father of lights, with whom is no variableness, neither shadow of turning." James 1:17.

The LORD puts in His people all they need to accomplish His work. What has the LORD put in you?

Discover Your Gift

The Bible says, "Wherefore he saith, When he ascended up on high, he led captivity captive, and gave gifts unto men." Ephesians 4:8. We will never understand all that God has given us until we give ourselves to the LORD. If you are a child of God, you have something to contribute. (Read again Corinthians 12:12-26.)   What can you do?

Dedicate Yourself And Your Gifts To God

The Bible says, "I beseech you therefore, brethren, by the mercies of God, that ye present your bodies a living sacrifice, holy, acceptable unto God, which is your reasonable service." Romans 12:1.

We all must choose who we will serve (Joshua 24:15). The best decision any child of God can make is to give their life to the LORD. This is how we dedicate our gifts and abilities to the LORD.

Develop Your Gifts

The Bible says, "Iron sharpeneth iron; so a man sharpeneth the countenance of his friend." Proverbs 27:17. We develop our gifts by getting around people who are sharper than we are. A great teacher can help a good teacher get better, a great singer can help a good singer get better, etc. Get around people who want you to be great.

Do Your Part

The Bible says, "But be ye doers of the word, and not hearers only, deceiving your own selves." James 1:22. When it is all said and done, we must be doers not just hearers. When I was a child, we had an expression, "There are too many chiefs and not enough Indians." Today we have too many chiefs and not enough believing doers. Be a doer!

Bezaleel had everything that he needed to accomplish God's will with his life. The will of God for Bezaleel was to help Moses do what God had called him to do. While in Egypt, the LORD put in Bezaleel the skill, knowledge, and ability to build the Tabernacle. God always puts His gifts for mankind in people. People are the real treasure in the LORD's work. Satan wants all the treasures of the LORD. He has been successful down through the ages with his threefold attack.

I have seen many gifted young men and women end their journey for God. In every case, it was in one of these three areas they failed. Paul said of our enemy, "...For we are not ignorant of his devices" II Corinthians 2:11. Bezaleel did not fall into the trap Satan set. Amen!

The only life that really counts is the one given to and for the LORD (Mark 8:35).

★ ★ ★ ★ ★

BEZALEEL JOINS THE INNER CIRCLE

Moses introduces Bezaleel to everyone and tells them that God has given Bezaleel to the great work of building the Tabernacle. Moses put some of his honor and influence on Bezaleel. The Bible says, "And Moses said unto the children of Israel, See, the LORD hath called by name Bezaleel the son of Uri, the son of Hur, of the tribe of Judah" Exodus 35:30. Without Moses' hand of blessing, Bezaleel wouldn't have had the success he had building the Tabernacle.

So, Bezaleel joins "Team Moses." Can you imagine being part of the Moses' inner circle? To be on the inside and to see and hear what Bezaleel was privileged to see and hear, would have been life changing. To work with this giant, in the faith, was an honor that few had.

The LORD Jesus had an inner circle. Peter, James, and John were His inner circle disciples. These three men heard the voice of God, they saw Moses and Elias, and they saw the LORD Jesus transfigured (Matthew 17:1-6). They saw and heard many things the rest of the disciples did not see and hear (Mark 5:37, 13:3; Luke 8:51).

★ ★ ★ ★ ★   79

Paul had an inner circle. Churches have an inner circle. Every man should seek to be an "inner circle" Christian. People who are part of the inner circle of a church are the ones who help make the church grow. They see what others do not see. The strength of the church is the inner circle.

How did Bezaleel join the inner circle? What did he do while being a part of the inner circle; and how can every man become an inner circle, Christian?

Moses Accepted Him

"And Moses said unto the children of Israel, See, the LORD hath called by name Bezaleel the son of Uri, the son of Hur, of the tribe of Judah" Exodus 35:30. Moses is repeating to the children of Israel what the LORD told him about Bezaleel. The Lord wants Bezaleel to stand with Moses in the great work that He has given him to do.

Moses understood that Bezaleel was not a Joshua or a Caleb. He knew that the LORD had given this young man a special gift that was needed in the LORD's work. If Moses does not accept him, then Bezaleel will not be able to do what God has called him to do.

The Golden Rule, in the work of the LORD, is to accept people for who they are and where they are. People are not all in the same place, in their walk with the LORD, and they are not all on the same level in their Christian service.

Moses Allowed Bezaleel To Be What God Made Him

"And he hath filled him with the spirit of God, in wisdom, in understanding, and in knowledge, and in all manner of workmanship" Exodus 35:31. Moses did not want or need Bezaleel to become another Moses. He needed him to be the best Bezaleel he could be.

Bezaleel was a craftsman. He was not Caleb. Caleb could teach you how to fight and to take a city. Bezaleel could teach you how to make the sword.

In the book of Esther, four different animals were used by the posts, to carry the message throughout the kingdom. They used "horses, mules, camels, and young dromedaries." Esther 8:10. Horses can go to nearby areas very quickly; mules can go up into mountains and down into valleys where horses cannot go; camels can carry heavy burdens great distances; but the dromedary can go great distances even faster. The dromedary can run eighteen hours a day.

It took all four kinds of animals to get the message to the people.

God gives us different kinds of people. It takes everyone working together to reach the world with the Gospel. Moses let Bezaleel be Bezaleel.

★ ★ ★ ★ ★

Bezaleel Taught Others What He Had Learned

The Bible says about Bezaleel, "And he (God) hath put in his heart that he may teach, both he, and Aholiab, the son of Ahisamach, of the tribe of Dan." Exodus 35:34. Moses allowed Bezaleel to teach others what he had been taught by the master craftsmen in Egypt.

The training and skillset, Bezaleel learned in Egypt, needed to be taught to all who wanted to be on the team.

God did not want Egyptians building His Tabernacle, but He did allow Bezaleel to learn from the Egyptians on how to make things right.

While Jesus was on earth, He taught His followers to let people, from many different backgrounds, find a place of service in God's plan for the ages. If we are to reach the world with the Gospel, we must do the same.

I have learned there are four groups of people, in every church, with whom we must work. Churches have leaders, workers, followers, and those to be reached.

Building The Inner-Circle Team

Leaders

Leaders have won personal victories; surrendered their lives to do God's will; stood with leadership; have an understanding about the work of the

LORD; maintain a good spirit; and they want to help the Pastor do what God has called him to do.

Leaders accept responsibility for the work of the LORD. Their lives challenge workers to do their best in the LORD's work. They are close to leadership and have a heart for people. They want the work to go forward. God puts in them the ability to do what He wants done in the work.

Leaders are the ones who have proven they are men and women of character and conviction. They are the ones who are close to God's man and must keep a good spirit.

They are also the ones who God will judge quickly, because the closer someone is to leadership, the more responsibility they have and will give an account of.

Leaders must love the Lord and do what they do because of their love for Christ. The Bible says, "For the love of Christ constraineth us." II Corinthians 5:14. In other words, it is their love for Christ that keeps them going.

They also must keep a thankful heart toward the one (the pastor) who has given them a place of leadership in the ministry.

I wrote in my Bible many years ago, "The will of God for my life is to help people do the will of God with their life." I believe one of the greatest things, a Christian can do with their life, is to

★ ★ ★ ★ ★ 83

help a pastor do what God has put in his heart to do.

Moses had something God had put in his heart to do, and Bezaleel gave his life to help him. Wow! What a precious gift God had given Moses. Leaders must love people and see their worth. Leaders will never be given gifted workers to help them if they fail to see the worth of every person.

Can you imagine having a team of gifted workers who have given their lives to help you do what the Lord has put in your heart to do? Jesus said, "For unto whomsoever much is given, of him shall be much required." Luke 12:48

Workers

Workers are those who have won personal victories; surrendered their lives to do God's will; understand the work and ministry of the local church; have the right spirit; and are faithful in their place of service.

Bezaleel was the leader who was over all the people that helped build the Tabernacle in the wilderness.

Bezaleel must have had a great spirit and a love for people. I say this because the people gave so much to Bezaleel, to build the Tabernacle, that Moses had to tell them to stop giving. The Bible says, "And Moses gave commandment, and they caused it to be proclaimed throughout the camp, saying, Let neither man nor woman make any more work for the offering of the sanctuary. So the people were restrained from bringing." Exodus 36:6.

People loved working with Bezaleel.

Workers are the ones who want to help the pastor in the local church ministries. They love and accept followers and work with them to win personal victories.

Followers

Followers are people who want to see the work move forward and who bring new people. Followers know who needs to be reached. They want to see their family and friends come to Christ.

Followers are those who know Christ as their personal Savior; have become members of the local church; and are winning personal victories.

Followers have a desire to see their friends and loved ones come to Christ. They know more unsaved people than leaders or workers do and will reach them if helped.

Our goal for a follower is to become a "Five Star Christian." This can be accomplished by doing these five things consistently: read your Bible, pray, be faithful to church, give, and tell others about Christ.

★ ★ ★ ★ ★

We have a world to reach.

Those to be reached are the people who have not become members of the local church. They could be saved or unsaved. Those to be reached cannot help until they become a part of the local church. Our desire is to see everyone saved and part of the church.

Pray for Laborers

Jesus said,

"The harvest truly is plenteous,

but the labourers are few;

Pray ye therefore the Lord of the harvest,

that he will send forth labourers into his harvest."

Matthew 9:37-38

How Can I Be Part Of The Inner Circle?

Put The Lord First In Your Life

Men who are part of the inner circle should say, "For to me to live is Christ, and to die is gain." Philippians 1:21.

★ ★ ★ ★ ★

Be a man who loves the Lord, and who is determined to please Him with your life. Be the right kind of person. The Bible says, "...If any man love God, the same is known of him." I Corinthians 8:3. Do people know you are a child of God and that you love the Lord? "Jesus said unto him, Thou shalt love the Lord thy God with all thy heart, and with all thy soul, and with all thy mind." Matthew 22:37.

Leaders want people close to them who know and love God and who have the right spirit. Leaders want to know, "...Is thine heart right, as my heart is with thy heart?" II Kings 10:15.

Have A Good Testimony Among the Brethren

Be a man God speaks about concerning leadership. The Bible says, "Wherefore, brethren, look ye out among you seven men of honest report, full of the Holy Ghost and wisdom, whom we may appoint over this business." Acts 6:3.

This is not just part of the qualifications for a deacon, but this should be the goal of every man. God speaks to us in many other portions of Scriptures about the men we should put in leadership. Determine to be the kind of man that God speaks about to lead.

Give Your Life To Do God's Will

"Jesus saith unto them, My meat is to do the will of him that sent me, and to finish his work." John 4:34. The Bible says, 'Wherefore be ye not unwise,

★ ★ ★ ★ ★

but understanding what the will of the Lord is." Ephesians 5:17. We will never know God's will for our life until we give our life to do God's will. The will of God for our life is to help people do the will of God with their life.

Be willing to help God's man do what God has given him to do with his life. We are all on a mission from God. Jesus said, "Go ye therefore, and teach all nations, baptizing them in the name of the Father, and of the Son, and of the Holy Ghost: Teaching them to observe all things whatsoever I have commanded you: and, lo, I am with you alway, even unto the end of the world. Amen." Matthew 28:19-20.

God holds pastors and church leaders accountable to reach the world with the Gospel. The church is on a mission from God. Our mission is to take the Gospel to every person. The Pastor of a church will one day give an account, to the LORD, for what the church has accomplished (Hebrews 13:17).

1. Getting the Gospel to as many people as possible. "The gospel must first be published among all nations." Mark 13:10.

2. Helping Christians have a good day at the Judgment Seat of Christ. "For we must all appear before the judgment seat of Christ; that everyone may receive the things done in his body, according to that he hath done, whether it be good or bad." II Corinthians 5:10.

Bezaleel, The Teacher

"And he hath put in his heart that he may teach, both he, and Aholiab, the son of Ahisamach, of the tribe of Dan." Exodus 35:34.

The LORD had called Moses to do something that is impossible for one man to do. He called him to build the Tabernacle. The building of the Tabernacle in the wilderness is going to require everyone's involvement.

Bezaleel is going to teach the children of Israel how to do what God has called them to do. He is their teacher. Thank the LORD for the people who teach others how to do the work of the LORD. The only way that truth goes from generation to generation is for someone to teach it. If we do not teach the next generation what we have been taught, it will be lost.

Bezaleel knew what to teach and he had a heart to teach people. Here are some questions to consider when thinking about teaching others.

Why Should We Teach Others?

The Bible says, "And his mercy is on them that fear him from generation to generation." Luke 1:50. We must teach, what we have been given, if the next generation is going to know God's mercy.

★ ★ ★ ★ ★   89

The first generation of believers were taught what David learned about God and His mercy. "For David, after he had served his own generation by the will of God, fell on sleep..." Acts 13:36.

The only way that truth goes from generation to generation is because someone is committed to teaching it. "...The righteousness of God revealed from faith to faith: as it is written, The just shall live by faith." Romans 1:17. What we believe is taught from generation to generation, from "faith to faith."

Bezaleel was not the first believer in his family's history, but he could have been the last one. If the generation that went before Bezaleel had failed to teach him what they had learned and been assured of about God, we would have never heard about Bezaleel. You may be the first believer in your family, but you can start a godly heritage.

IADOM

There was a sign, in a factory, during World War II that read, "IADOM." A leader in the war effort saw the sign and was puzzled about what it meant. He could not understand the meaning of the word IADOM. The sign was posted in every part of the factory in big letters.

Finally, he asked a young lady what the odd spelling meant. She said, "You don't know what IADOM means?" He said, "No, I have been trying to figure it out all day." She told him, "It was put on the walls in this weapons factory when our nation went to war. It is a daily reminder that helps us do our best and continue to do our part to win the victory. The letters IADOM stand for, "It All Depends On Me."

She said, "We all believe that what we are doing here is making a difference in our fight for freedom."

Who Are We To Teach?

The Bible says, "And the things that thou hast heard of me among many witnesses, the same commit thou to faithful men, who shall be able to teach others also." II Timothy 2:2. We are to teach faithful men. Men, who have proven themselves to be faithful, are to be prepared by the generation that has gone on before them.

Every man is to pass on to the next generation what he has been given. Find a faithful man and invest your life in him. Paul said about the ones who invested their lives in him, "I thank my God upon every remembrance of you... because I have you in my heart." Philippians 1:3,7. Who will be saying they thank God for every remembrance of us after we are gone?

What Are We To Teach?

The Bible says we are to teach the next generation, "And they continued stedfastly in the apostles' doctrine and fellowship, and in breaking of bread, and in prayers." Acts 2:42.

★ ★ ★ ★ ★

According to Jesus we are to teach "them to observe all things whatsoever I have commanded you." Matthew 28:20. We are to teach the "...same..." that we have been taught (II Timothy 2:2). We trace our spiritual heritage back to the apostles' doctrine. We are continuing today in the apostles' doctrine.

The Scriptural doctrine that we have been given is the same Scriptural doctrine we are to teach.

How Are We To Teach?

We are to follow the examples we have been handed down through the centuries. Jesus said, "For I have given you an example, that ye should do as I have done to you." John 13:15. We are to teach by example. We are the only Bible that some people will ever read. Paul said, "Let no man despise thy youth; but be thou an example of the believers, in word, in conversation, in charity, in spirit, in faith, in purity." I Timothy 4:12.

- In word = Let the Word of God be the final authority.

- In conversation = Let the words of our mouth be pleasing to the Lord.

- In charity = Have a heart for people (compassion).

- In spirit = Keep a good spirit about the things of the LORD.

- In purity = Live above reproach.

Teach The Next Generation

"And these words, which I command thee this day, shall be in thine heart: And thou shalt teach them diligently unto thy children..."

Deuteronomy 6:6-7

What Is The Most Important Thing About Teaching?

How We Teach is Important

The Bible says, "And he (Jesus) taught them many things by parables, and said unto them in his doctrine" Mark 4:2.

The LORD Jesus used many methods of teaching. He used stories (parables); He used children; He used birds, rocks, flowers trees; He "...taught the people out of the ship..." (Luke 5:3); He was the Master teacher. He is our example.

Every teacher should want to improve his methods of teaching. How we teach is important.

What We Teach Is More Important

The Bible says, "...The people were astonished at his doctrine: For he taught them as one having authority, and not as the scribes." Matthew 7:28b-29. People need to be taught the Word of God and the doctrine that we have been given.

★ ★ ★ ★ ★   93

The LORD Jesus knew that what people believe determines how they live. Doctrine is our foundation of belief. Paul said, "...Thou hast fully known my doctrine, manner of life..." II Timothy 3:10. What he believed ("...my doctrine..."), determined how he lived ("...my manner of life..."). What we teach is more important.

How We Live Is The Most Important

People who teach the next generation should be men and women of character.

- **Honest** "...Look ye out among you...men of honest report..." Acts 6:3.

- **Devout** "And one Ananias, a devout man according to the law, having a good report of all the Jews which dwelt there" Acts 22:12.

- **Good Testimony** "Moreover he must have a good report of them which are without; lest he fall into reproach and the snare of the devil." I Timothy 3:7.

- **Good Men Filled With the Spirit of God** "For he was a good man, and full of the Holy Ghost and of faith: and much people was added unto the Lord." Acts 11:24.

These verses help us to see that men who are to serve the LORD must live right. One of the highest compliments that can be paid to a man is, "He is a good man." Bezaleel was a good man, and he was a good teacher.

We Remember You

We remember you from the days of our youth,

You were the ones who taught us knowledge and truth.

You were the ones who helped us be part of the team,

You were the ones who were always kind and never mean.

You were the ones who took us by the hand,

You were the ones who helped us to be strong and stand.

You were the ones who never gave up on girls and boys,

You were the ones who taught us to love people not toys.

You were the ones who corrected us when we did wrong,

You were the ones who made us join in and get along.

You were the ones who saw the twinkle in our eye,

You were the ones who believed one day we would fly.

You were the ones who encouraged us to continue on,

You were the ones who helped us live life with a song.

You were the ones who believed for every life there's a plan,

You were the ones who showed faith in our fellow man.

You are the ones who now cheer us from the bleachers,

You are the ones we lovingly call our teachers.

"I thank my God upon every remembrance of you."

Dedicated To All Who Teach Our Youth TS

★ ★ ★ ★ ★

★ ★ ★ ★ ★

Bezaleel, Finished And Approved

"And Bezaleel the son of Uri, the son of Hur, of the tribe of Judah, made all that the LORD commanded Moses...Thus was all the work of the tabernacle of the tent of the congregation finished: and the children of Israel did according to all that the LORD commanded Moses, so did they." Exodus 38:22; 39:32.

It is amazing that this "...mixed multitude..." that came out of Egypt has accomplished such a powerful work for God. Who would have believed it? The Tabernacle is finished, and now it will be dedicated to the LORD and the fire will come down. I am sure that one day we will feel the same about what this generation of believers has accomplished.

God told Moses that He would come down (Exodus 3:8) and deliver His people. Moses took the people out of Egypt to "...meet with God..." Exodus 19:17.

The purpose of this Tabernacle is to provide a place where the LORD can meet with people. He said, "And there I will meet with the children of Israel, and the tabernacle shall be sanctified by my glory." Exodus 29:43. The Tabernacle is finished and approved.

★ ★ ★ ★ ★

(Every serious-minded believer should be familiar with the Tabernacle in the wilderness, a subject I love to speak on, but in these lessons, I have limited myself.)

Bezaleel Finished What God Gave Him To Do

The Bible says, "And Bezaleel the son of Uri, the son of Hur, of the tribe of Judah, made all that the LORD commanded Moses." Exodus 38:22. We spend a lot of time celebrating what people start. The LORD wants us to have a good ending.

The Children of Israel Finished The Work God Gave Them To Do

The Bible says, "Thus was all the work of the tabernacle of the tent of the congregation finished: and the children of Israel did according to all that the LORD commanded Moses, so did they." Exodus 39:32. They accomplished something with their lives that all the generations to follow could enjoy.

Their life's work made it possible for the generations to come to have a place to meet with God.

Moses Approves The Finished Work

The Bible says, "And Moses did look upon all the work, and, behold, they had done it as the LORD had commanded, even so had they done it: and Moses blessed them." Exodus 39:43. Moses sees, on this earth, the finished work of what God had put in his heart and mind to do.

The Bible says, "...And Moses blessed them..." Think about what that blessing meant to the children of Israel and to Bezaleel. Great people are thankful people, and Moses knew how to say "Thank You.

How Did This Mixed Multitude Do It?

They Followed God's Plan

"According to all that the LORD commanded Moses, so the children of Israel made all the work." Exodus 39:42. The Tabernacle was built "... according to..." God's plan. If we want to see the work of the LORD accomplished, we must work according to God's plan. (Matthew 28:19-20; Mark 16:15; Acts 1:8)

They Followed Moses, God's Man

The Bible says, "And Moses did look upon all the work, and, behold, they had done it as the LORD had commanded, even so had they done it: and Moses blessed them." Exodus 39:43. Moses is God's man, and the LORD had given him what the people needed.

If a person is not a good follower, they will not one day be a good leader. Paul said to the church at Thessalonica, "And ye became followers of us, and of the Lord..." I Thessalonians 1:6.

★ ★ ★ ★ ★

They Worked Together as a Team

We read, "...And the children of Israel did..." v.32. God does not call each one by name. He just says, "...The children of Israel made all the work" v. 42. Big shots are not team players. It has been said over and over, but it is true.

TEAM spells:

Together

Everyone

Accomplishes

More

Be a team player.

They Used the Resources God Gave Them

The Bible says, "And they spake unto Moses, saying, The people bring much more than enough for the service of the work, which the LORD commanded to make." Exodus 36:5. The people gave so much that Moses had to tell them to quit giving (v. 36). Amazingly, that is not the case today. Today we have a generation of believers who try to make all they can and keep all they make. Nothing great for God will ever be accomplished without making a real sacrifice.

Remember it is never money that we need. The great need in the work of the LORD is people; "... the labourers are few...." We need people who will give what the LORD has put in their hands.

They Used the Treasure They Brought from Egypt

The Bible says, "And they received of Moses all the offering, which the children of Israel had brought for the work of the service of the sanctuary, to make it withal. And they brought yet unto him free offerings every morning...For the stuff they had was sufficient for all the work to make it, and too much." Exodus 36:3,7.

They did not hold back. God always puts in His children's hands everything needed for His work. We are stewards of God's wealth.

They Used the Time God Gave Them

They went to work "...every morning." v. 3. Every day there was something to do. Time is our personal treasure. It takes time to build something for the LORD.

They Used their God-given Talent

The Bible says, "And all the wise men, that wrought all the work of the sanctuary, came every man from his work which they made." Exodus 36:4. Everyone did what they could, and at what they were gifted. Our gifts and abilities are given to us for two reasons - first, to provide for our families and second, to provide for the LORD's work.

They Finished What God Gave Them To Do

The Bible says, "Better is the end of a thing than the beginning thereof: and the patient in spirit is better than the proud in spirit." Ecclesiastes 7:8. How are you going to finish? My beloved pastor, Dr. Lee Roberson, would often remind me that the three most difficult things to do in the Christian life is:

- Keep Your Life Right With God and Other Believers

- Stay On Track With God's Plan For Your Life

- Stay Excited About What The Lord Has Given You To Do

I wrote a humorous story about people, I have known, who got mad and quit before their life's work was finished.

I Got Mad and Quit Today

Some humor dedicated to all who think too highly of themselves.

"For I say, through the grace given unto me, to every man that is among you not to think of _himself_ more highly than he ought to think; but to think soberly, according as God hath dealt to every man the measure of faith." Romans 12:3.

I got mad and quit today and threw more than my future away. I grew tired of the way people were treating me, I'm important, is that so hard to see?

I know that some think I am a foolish man, but every once in a while, you have to take a stand! Especially when things don't go your way, and you start having problems every day; when no one notices all that you do, and at times they even criticize you; don't stay around even for a benefit, throw a fit and quit.

Step back and see what they can do, now that they don't have you. Live your life the way you please, work hard or be at ease, play some golf or fish awhile, just do what makes you smile. They will soon know that you were right, it may take some time, or it could happen overnight.

Everyone will want you back when the work stops or gets off track. Just sit back and enjoy the mess, they will soon learn that you were the best.

And when you see Jesus, He will understand. Go ahead and tell Him what happened to you by man, why He may even show you the nail prints in His hands.

But when you see all that could have been, had you lived your life according to His plan, when those you knew are cast into the pit, you will remember the day that you got mad and quit.

So, come back to God while you have the time, find your place on the firing line. Die to self and determine to stay true, the work of the Lord has a place for you. One day we will be with Jesus beyond the blue, that day you'll see; He has a crown awaiting you.

Remember, "none of us liveth to himself, and no man dieth to himself...Therefore, my beloved brethren, be ye stedfast, unmoveable, always

★ ★ ★ ★ ★

abounding in the work of the Lord, forasmuch as ye know that your labour is not in vain in the Lord." Romans 14:7 & I Corinthians 15:58

The saddest words ever penned:

"It Could Have Been"

Jesus said, "If thou hadst known, even thou, at least in this thy day, the things which belong unto thy peace! but now they are hid from thine eyes."

Luke 19:42

God Loves You

"For God so loved the world, that He gave His only begotten Son, that whosoever believeth in Him should not perish, but have everlasting life" John 3:16.

This great Bible verse reveals four truths from the heart of God for all people.

We Are Loved.

God wants us to know that **we are loved**. The Lord Jesus said, "For God so loved the world...." You are a part of this world, and God loves you. He gave His Son for you, and He wants you "...to know the love of Christ..." Ephesians 3:19.

We Are Of Worth.

The Lord also wants us to know that **we are of worth**. We are so dear to God "...that He gave His only begotten Son...." The Bible teaches us that we are all sinners. "For all have sinned, and come short of the glory of God" Romans 3:23. And sin must be paid for. "For the wages of sin is death..." Romans 6:23.

But the Bible also teaches us that "...Christ died for our sins according to the scriptures" I Corinthians 15:3. God demonstrated His love for us

★★★★★ 105

and our worth to Him when He sent His Son to die in our place. The good news is that the Lord Jesus paid our sin debt in full when He died on the cross. "For He hath made Him to be sin for us…" II Corinthians 5:21.

Christ loved us and gave Himself for us as payment for our sin. You may ask, "How can God forgive my sin?" He can because of what Jesus did. "…While we were yet sinners, Christ died for us" Romans 5:8.

We Can Have Hope.

God wants us to know that **we can have hope**. He said "…that whosoever believeth in Him should not perish…."

Life is fragile, and people are perishing. But Christ came "…that they might have life, and that they might have it more abundantly" John 10:10. In a world where so many have lost hope, God wants us to know that the "…Lord Jesus Christ…is our hope" I Timothy 1:1. He rose from the dead, and He said, "…Because I live, ye shall live also" John 14:19.

We Can Have Purpose.

God wants us to know that we can have purpose in life. He desires that we "…should not perish but have everlasting life." "And this is the promise that He hath promised us, even eternal life" I John 2:25. You may ask, "How can I receive God's promise of eternal life?"

★ ★ ★ ★ ★

Acknowledge that you are a sinner, "for all have sinned, and come short of the glory of God" Romans 3:23.

Believe that the Lord Jesus died for you, for "Christ died for our sins according to the scriptures" I Corinthians 15:3.

Call upon the Lord to save you, "for whosoever shall call upon the name of the Lord shall be saved" Romans 10:13.

If you would be willing to turn to Christ in repentance and faith, pray this simple prayer of salvation:

"LORD, I know that I am a sinner, and I believe You died and rose again for me. I trust You to forgive me. Come into my heart and save me. Deliver me from my sin and help me to live for You. In Jesus' name, Amen."

The Lord Jesus said, "...I give unto them eternal life; and they shall never perish..." John 10:28. Everlasting life is ours when we receive Christ as our personal Saviour.

Now That You are A Christian:

- Share your new-found faith with your family and friends. Acts 16:31-33.

- Identify with Christ through believer's baptism and become part of a local, Bible-believing church. Acts 2:41-47.

★ ★ ★ ★ ★   107

Joy In Heaven

"I say unto you, there is joy in the presence of the angels of God over one sinner that repenteth."

Luke 15:10

How To Be A Man Like Bezaleel

"And the LORD spake unto Moses, saying, See, I have called by name Bezaleel the son of Uri, the son of Hur, of the tribe of Judah: And I have filled him with the spirit of God, in wisdom, and in understanding, and in knowledge, and in all manner of workmanship, To devise cunning works, to work in gold, and in silver, and in brass, And in cutting of stones, to set them, and in carving of timber, to work in all manner of workmanship... and in the hearts of all that are wise hearted I have put wisdom, that they may make all that I have commanded thee;" Exodus 31:1-6.

Bezaleel was a gift from God to Moses. He is also a man, in whom we see how God prepares people with what they need to advance the work of the Lord, in this world. The name Bezaleel can be interpreted as "in the shadow of God" or "under divine protection."

Bezaleel was what we refer to as a layman. He was chosen to carry out a divine work of God. Everything about his life, in Egypt, was a preparation for the mission God has chosen for him. Bezaleel was much more than an artist or a master craftsman. He was a prodigy.

★★★★★ 109

The Bible says, "I will praise thee; for I am fearfully and wonderfully made: marvellous are thy works; and that my soul knoweth right well." Psalm 139:14.

Understanding the life and work of Bezaleel helps us to believe God has a generation of gifted followers who are waiting to hear their call.

May the Lord give us an army of Bezaleels to advance the Gospel to all nations. I challenge men, who know God, to become a man like Bezaleel. Determine to be a man like Bezaleel. You ask, "How can I become a man like Bezaleel?"

B - Be a Believer

God said, "...I have filled him with the spirit of God..." Exodus 31:3. You must first be a believer. Only believers are filled with the Holy Spirit. The Bible says, "These things have I written unto you that believe on the name of the Son of God; that ye may know that ye have eternal life, and that ye may believe on the name of the Son of God." I John 5:13. Are you a believer?

We read where "believers were the more added to the Lord, multitudes both of men and women" Acts 5:14. Bezaleel was a man of faith. If there is any doubt about your Salvation, nail it down. The Bible says, "And he that doubteth is damned if he eat, because he eateth not of faith: for whatsoever is not of faith is sin." Romans 14:23.

It has been said, "Living with doubt is like having rubber crutches, they will let you down when you need them."

There was no doubt, Bezaleel knew God, because God filled him with the "Spirit of God."

E – Empty Self

God said, "...I have filled him..." Exodus 31:3. God cannot fill what is already full. We must empty ourselves of the things that take the place of the LORD.

The Bible says, "Love not the world, neither the things that are in the world. If any man love the world, the love of the Father is not in him. For all that is in the world, the lust of the flesh, and the lust of the eyes, and the pride of life, is not of the Father, but is of the world. And the world passeth away, and the lust thereof: but he that doeth the will of God abideth for ever." I John 2:15-17.

- God takes what you give Him.

- He cleanses what He takes.

- He fills what He has cleansed.

- He uses what He has filled.

Z – Zeal for God's Work

Desire is the engine that drives the Christian life. The Bible tells us that "Bezaleel...made all that

★★★★★

the LORD commanded Moses." Exodus 38:22. He finished what Moses needed him to do, and his desire helped others finish strong.

Desire and zeal are the things that fuel the Christian life. Nothing has ever been accomplished, for God, without zeal and desire for the work of the LORD.

The psalmist said, "For the zeal of thine house hath eaten me up..." Psalm 69:9. When is the last time we heard a child of God say they are eaten up with desire and zeal for the Lord's work?

Paul reminded Timothy not to let desire die in his life. He said, "Wherefore I put thee in remembrance that thou stir up the gift of God, which is in thee by the putting on of my hands." II Timothy 1:6.

Peter said, "Yea, I think it meet, as long as I am in this tabernacle, to stir you up by putting you in remembrance...beloved, I now write unto you; in both which I stir up your pure minds by way of remembrance." II Peter 1:13,3:1.

A – Advance the Cause of Christ

Moses is taking the next step in Gods' plan for Israel, by building the Tabernacle where God can meet with His people. "But I would ye should understand, brethren, that the things which happened unto me have fallen out rather unto the furtherance of the gospel." Philippians 1:12.

When it is all said and done, about our life, will people say that we've advanced the cause of Christ with our life and ministry?

The only way to advance the cause of Christ is to give your life to help people do the will of God with their life.

L – Love People and See their Worth

Jesus said, "By this shall all men know that ye are my disciples, if ye have love one to another." John 13:35. It is true that people do not care how much you know, until they know how much you care.

Men who make a difference are men who love people and see their worth. Bezaleel was a man unknown by most people but, he was a gifted treasure for Moses. Bezaleel loved people and helped them do something great with their life.

E – Equip Others to Serve

God gives church leaders, "For the perfecting of the saints, for the work of the ministry, for the edifying of the body of Christ." Ephesians 4:12. Take the time to train and help people. Invest your life in the next generation.

The Bible says, "For none of us liveth to himself, and no man dieth to himself." Romans 14:10. Every life touches another life. We all have been touched by others, for we have their labor in us.

★ ★ ★ ★ ★

E – Encourage Someone Every Day

The Bible says, "But exhort one another daily, while it is called To day; lest any of you be hardened through the deceitfulness of sin." Hebrews 3:13. One of the daily duties of a child of God is to encourage someone every day.

Most people need a pat on the back and to hear, "That a boy" to keep going for the LORD. Our encouragement could make the difference in someone going forward for the LORD or turning his back on the LORD.

L – Look Up

The Bible says, "Looking unto Jesus the author and finisher of our faith; who for the joy that was set before him endured the cross, despising the shame, and is set down at the right hand of the throne of God." Hebrews 12:2. We are looking forward to our coming King. This generation of believers is closer to the coming of Christ than any other generation that has ever lived.

Keep looking up!

★ ★ ★ ★ ★

For more helpful information and free downloads visit

www.FiveStarChristianMinistries.com